On Becoming Rose

Carina Rose

On Becoming Rose

Carina Rose

PELICAN
PUBLISHERS

Kingston, Jamaica

PELICAN
PUBLISHERS

INNOVATE • CREATE • COMMUNICATE

First Published in Jamaica, 2019 by Pelican Publishers Limited

19 Balmoral Avenue,
Kingston 10, Jamaica, W.I
Tel: (876) 978-8377 Fax: (876) 978-0048
Email: info@pelicanpublishers.com
Website: www.pelicanpublishers.com

© Carina Rose

ISBN: 978-976-8240-96-5

Cover Design by Pelican Graphics

Book Design and Layout by Pelican Graphics

Table of Contents

Acknowledgement

I would like to acknowledge everyone who played a role in my academic and/or creative accomplishments. Special mention to my mother, who always supported my talents and visions, and Minister Gordon, who like a father, always saw the beauty and purpose of pain. He always believed in me and pressured me into carrying out my purpose.

Introduction

On Becoming Rose is a life-experience travelogue. It is about welcoming spiritual and professional advancement, having been through the process of growing up and the pains and joys that comes with that. It explores the writer's childhood to adulthood experiences - the good and the bad and the lessons learnt. Of course, no journey is ever truly travelled alone, so some of the experiences shared belong to others with whom the writer have come in contact with - for better or worse. The book is raw truth. In it, the author embraces imperfections, yearns to be loved the right way, prepares for womanhood, accepts maturity, gives advice to her future son.

The purpose of the book is to tell a story, to impact the lives of those who need to tell their truths and are fearful, to inspire and to teach.

Red Petals in my Hands

I have never experienced love
And I always wanted
To be able to touch it
Feel it
Hold it
Hold on to it
Identify it
To be able to bask in its presence
And all its glory

I grew up in a place where love was hardly
expressed
We knew it was there but it was never uttered
Always hanging on the tip of our tongues
Waiting to fall off
Waiting to be acknowledged

Probably waiting for you to open your arms
Or lend a listening ear

For me to apologize
For her to move on

For you to say baby I was wrong -
Forgive me
Forgive me for causing you pain
Forgive me for not being the same
Forgive me for playing

I promised to show you love
But it seems I don't know love
I don't know what love is
But I've always been interested to find out
To be able to touch it
Feel it
Hold it
Hold on to it like the red petals in my hands

It's the Little Things

Always appreciate time, space and silence

Appreciate the fact that sometimes you never
know what's going to happen next

Always appreciate the fact that you don't
always have the right answers

Appreciate small pockets of laughter

Appreciate smiling faces

Appreciate that not all smiling faces will take
you places

Appreciate true friendship, risks, mistakes, the
love that never last

Appreciate all the things that happened
in your past

Appreciate the move

Appreciate changes

Appreciate the fact that growth comes in
stages

Free

I am free
I am free in my mind, body and soul
I'm free as free is so powerful, so bold

Free to write this piece on an antiquated wall
Free to let thoughts and aspirations dance on
this crumpled paper

Free as the plaits in my hair disentangle in the
wind
Free as free can be in my own black skin.

Becoming a Woman... the Transition

As I crossed the street from the grocery shop
Something trickled down my right thigh
And my stomach felt a foreign feeling
As though a ton of bricks had landed right
inside

I ran hurriedly inside the yard
Mommy told me this would happen
But I didn't know the day would come so soon

Dropped the bag; Eggs cracked
Knocked over bottles on the dining table
Arrived inside the private room
Pulled down my shorts

ON BECOMING ROSE

And there it was ...
Mommy!!!

And she ran quickly to my rescue
To provide me with protection

I no longer climb the trees
Or play certain games with the boys on the
road
Could not stop and say hi to old Jimmy ...
Without feeling awkward

I kept folding my arms
Hiding the two blossoms ...
Hoping no one could stare
Childhood was yesterday
Womanhood was now here

I had to prepare.

My First Slow Dance

What ever happened to slow dances and long
conversations?
Bonfires and candle light dinners?

I had my first slow dance when I was 24
And for the first time, the very first time I felt
so loved!
I wasn't given material things
Nor was it sexual
But it was that one dance
A dance with a gentleman

So magical

I feared his touch at first
My heart was beating very fast
when he held me close
But the look he gave me

ON BECOMING ROSE

Allowed me to trust him
It was an older man
Could have been my father
Pulling me inwards then outwards
Then in again

As we danced close I realized
That what was missing in my life ...
Was a dance with my very own father.

Empowerment

There is something that the club does to me
No other place has that strong effect on my
spirit
When I step in the club I feel strong and
powerful
All eyes looking at me as I enter
Wanting me to be a part of the team

When I see the ladies
dancing on the stage
on the pole
I emulate them
I aspire to be them
As they create art with their bodies

As they bend and
Form different shapes
In their heels.
As they bend their curves
Oh what curves do some of them have

ON BECOMING ROSE

I see a gymnast
I see me doing what they do ..
And all eyes are on me

I see men and women go up to tip them
And they move their bodies
So sensually
Effortlessly

To collect their pay.

The Rush

What made me fall in love with him
in the first place
Was the rush ...
We made through the door
To the the kitchen counter
Juices running down my thighs
Escaping guilt
And dripping on the floor

The rush I made as he blessed my heavens
And I climbed his Mount Everest
Was his name

The rush I made when my vocal cords
Could hold the note no longer
And produced an unending scream
The rush of the blood flowing to the veins
Standing in my neck
And in his manhood ...
9 inch pistol
Dangerous yet satisfying

ON BECOMING ROSE

As it made my waters rise
Squishing, squashing
Making funny noises
Hyperventilating
My body is contemplating
its next move

What made me fall in love with him
was the rush
The rush I made squeezing his neck
Scraping his back
The rush I made as I sprinkled the room
The rush that I released.

Normal is Boring

❦

I am not normal
and I can live with that
because similar isn't different
and where's the fun in that?

❦

Dear Daddy

They say you're my daddy
But I only bear your surname
I can't say I know you and
I'm sure you can only say the same

I wish you were there to protect me
in the streets
Teach me right from wrong
Give me the talk about the birds
and the bees...
Be my daddy - big and strong !

I wish you were there to screen all the guys
before I go on dates
and to even scare some of them so we'd not..

I wish you were there to be strict
telling me 'You're not going out

looking like that!'
I wish you were there to tell me
'that that guy is too old for you and
you will end up hurt'

I wish you were there to treat me
like a princess
and give me anything I want
I wish you could protect me from the crooks
on the road
I wish you could tell me at age 16 that I
couldn't have a bf until I'm 40
And that you didn't tolerate certain lifestyles...

I wish you were there to call me
on my birthday
And throw me a birthday party
Tell me how much you love me
And how you really care
Oh daddy; I just really, really wish
You were actually there!

While Being the Other Woman

How it feels to know that you can never have
him
All the silent kisses and the fingers touching
your heavens
in secret
Will never count
at all

You'll never meet his mama
And you'll never meet his daughter
So why bother?
You can never invite him over for Sunday
dinner

You can never have him to yourself for
valentine's day or Christmas Day
New Year's Eve you're busy finding someone
else to text because he'll be out with her

Relationship dressed in whispers
A love expressed behind
Closed doors
and
Window sills
Behind curtains
and
Walls so high
That if you scream
No one will hear

He hides and sleeps with you
He hides to sleep with you
He hides...
Sometimes you have to keep quiet while he's
on the phone
you dare not say a word
If you want to keep this tryst going

Oh but you get to meet the friends though
Oh but you experience his chill spots

ON BECOMING ROSE

He shows you his favorite restaurant
His barbershop
Oh but you get the long conversations and
the multiple text messages
Especially when he is outside playing football
Or heading to the grocery store
or plain and simple, when he is on the road

Oh but you get the 'how are you' and 'are u
ok' check-ups
He tries...
So why complain?
As I write this piece I'm drinking a glass of
Pinot Grigio
I'm wearing lace and black stilettos
Because I borrowed him today
and we turned my place into one hot mess

Can I get a towel?
How do I look?
"Do I look like a man who just cheated on his
woman?
I stood there
Couldn't move
Somehow courage found me and propelled
my tongue to say

"You look fine"

And in that moment

In that sad moment

All I wanted him to do was leave

Oh how it feels to know he can only make you

half-happy.

Mama's Sweet Tea

It used to be an awesome feeling
Mama combing my hair
Her warm hands parting my mane
Running through my scalp
As a child

Even now as an adult
I love having her comb my hair
Brush my tresses
It is pampering
An expression of love
Even if she doesn't say I love you"
I know she loves me

Mama usually curled my hair
Braided my hair
Placed extensions in my hair
Washed my hair

Towel-dried my hair
Dyed my hair

I felt like I was her baby all over again

You could tell by the look of her fingers
Coarse yet beautiful
That she is a hardworking woman

Since mama migrated
I get up every morning
And curl my own hair
Sometimes I get it right
Sometimes I don't

I didn't even know I had it in me to curl my
own hair
On the days it came out right
God bless my mama
The lady with the gifted heart and hands

My Imperfections

Sometimes I am not easy to talk to
I can be hard to handle
I cry for the simplest of things
I frown when I don't get my way

If you're lucky, I might not throw a tantrum.
I still bite my nails when I'm nervous
I still feel insecure even when I know
You think I'm the prettiest woman in the room

I have anger problems
Sometimes I'm sure I am bi-polar
All of these imperfections make me worry that
one day
One sunny, rainy, cloudy or windy day
You may up and leave.

From Pain to Power

Do you remember...
When we bridged the light?
When we had no kitchen
So we put a table outside to wash the plates
When we only had one bed
So my place was on the floor ...

Do you remember
When we went days without light
We had to buy candles every night
Not even water
So Rosie would push her hose through the
zinc sheets
That our buckets and pans could be filled
Water to bathe, wash the dishes and
fill our cups
Until they overflowed...

ON BECOMING ROSE

Do you remember
How we use to buy the big gil of oil
and the quarter bread
and ice from the lady up the road

Do you remember
When I was out of a job for 6 months
and my boyfriend was verbally abusive
and controlling

Do you remember
When I was diagnosed with anaemia
and lost so much weight
I was in pain for weeks
Bed-ridden

Do you remember mama?

Oh mama we knew pain
We knew struggles
And we knew what it meant to fight
And we did what we had to do to survive

Who would've thought that on March 16, 2016
You would've soared
like you never soared before
Who would've thought that humans could fly
Who gave you so much power, mama?

The Big Chop

They say that when a woman balds her head
It means something
Not just she's getting tired
Of dealing with the length of her hair
But something deeper than that
'Your hair is your beauty'
I was told while growing up

But when a man grows his hair
He doesn't do it because he wants to feel
beautiful
And when he cuts it, is there any real
significance?
But when a woman cuts her hair, she's
shedding.
She's shedding old life, old ways, old mistakes
She's shedding hurt, regrets, pain...

When a woman balds her head
It takes her back to the very first time
When her body started to prepare
her for womanhood
As the walls of her uterus shed and bleed on a
monthly cycle

When a woman balds her head it says
she's over it.
She has been down that road before.
She came. She saw. She conquered.

It means she's mighty, fearless and
aware of self.
She's not her hair.
She had the courage to take risks
And to prove that she's even beautiful ..
Even without it.
When a woman balds her head, it means
something.

Not just that she's getting tired
Of dealing with the length of her hair
But something deeper than that.

We Grow

We grow every day.
No, not necessarily physically
But gaining knowledge
And learning from our mistakes.

We grow you and I
Together and apart
Apart and together.
We are not perfect
And never will be.

But we grow
to love
to talk
to laugh
Even though sometimes my cheeks
put up a fight just to go up.

We grow like a plant springing from its roots
And creating flowers for birds and bees
To feed on
And extract sweet, sweet nectar.

And sometimes we only grow to grow apart.

I Named my Daughter Melanin

Little black girls

Frolicking on the playground

Dancing in the autumn air

Embracing innocence

I adore you

Your melanin is power

It speaks volumes

It radiates a room

Your coils

Your curls

The kink in your hair is like no other

Your thick lips

Your wide nose

Is like no other

If I had a little black girl
I would call her Melanin
Because she would be symbolic of black
Consciousness and represent a tower of
strength
She would be an inspiration to all the little
black girls

And she would read books and learn the
language of
Our people
She would learn the history of our people
The segregated parts
Chopped into tiny pieces
Destroyed

She would learn why her race is being
depleted
She would learn the songs
Poems and dances
Of our forefathers

But sometimes I wonder if your name
will shut doors
On you
Doors for opportunities

ON BECOMING ROSE

Doors that behind them you might have to
Straighten your coil and the kink in your hair
Doors that will probably force you
To get your nose
Straight
Doors that will thin your lips
And thicken your butt
I hope those doors won't shut
Because of your name ...

Melanin.

The Peace they Stole from Me

It was like stale air in an unopened room
All of a sudden your juices became unpleasant
Your head seemed a bit bigger
Your manhood was 3 inches smaller
Your feet even broader than they were before

Unfamiliar with the absence of pain, I was
unable to identify its presence

Suddenly I know what bathing in a bathroom
feels like
No more bath pans
Suddenly I know what eating around a dinner
table feels like
Suddenly I had my own room
No more sleeping on sponges placed on a

floor

But a bed ...

Yes a bed

No longer had to stay up until 5am

So that my step-father couldn't try to touch

me at nights

Suddenly I didn't have to grow up too fast

Because suddenly

I was at peace

Suddenly I now know what stillness feels like

I can now understand the meaning of

relaxation

Suddenly I know what a hug feels like

Because suddenly

I found PEACE!

That Moment: The Mary Jane in Me

That moment you're scrolling through your
Whatsapp contact list
About to message a guy and play it off like
It's an accident
Because you need a guy to talk to
Desperate for some attention

That moment you blocked all the good
looking guys on Whatsapp
Because they all turned out to be jerks

That moment when you wonder if any of the
guys who you usually take forever to reply to
their messages were ever good looking
That moment when you've been waiting on
your male best friend to confess and say

'I've liked you too...'
That moment when you ask your friend if her
bf doesn't have any single friends or
Good looking brothers

That moment when you start flirting with
someone you don't even want
But you flirt - trying to convince yourself that
you still got it

That moment when you start being nice to the
guy that used to annoy the hell outta you

That moment when you told yourself you
would never talk to a guy that lives with his
Baby Momma and poof! There you go again...

That moment when you start to question if
you're still beautiful and wonder why
"The Perfect Guy" hasn't approached your
door step yet.

That moment when the woman in you
questions self...
Should I wait or should I make a move?

25

Twenty fine

Mid point

The centre of attraction

Just like the middle-finger

Half-way there

Split between

The in-between

The bridge between

the 20s and the 30s

It was the year of my life when I found myself

Alone

It was the age I became a woman

Discovered things about me I never knew

existed

Fell in love with self

Unraveled God's purpose

Climbed mountains I never climbed

ON BECOMING ROSE

Fought the devil in my sleep
Crossed rivers that were so deep
Rivers of lessons to guide my daughter
Brother
My sisters
Oh sister
Take life one step at a time
Do good to others even when they have
wronged you
Be your brother's keeper
And your sisters too.

Preparation

I've been up since 5am...
A cockroach crawled on my leg
I jumped up in shock
Quickly brushed it off
It landed on the wall
I used my slipper and hit him so hard
Hit it again jus fi ensure seh it dead
But I didn't understand what it meant

Stood over it and thought "this is it"
I've had enough
I've had it up to my neck
Time to speak
Time to voice my concern
Time to let go
Time to walk away

Time for a change
Time to stand for something

Or fall for anything
Time to let things go
Time to let newness creep in

Time to make a decision
Time to stop procrastinating
Time to stop being indecisive
Time to leave the old ways behind
Time to clear the clutter
Time to make time
Time for the cleanse.

Doors Opened

I see the glossiness in her eyes
Every time I look at her, I smile
Not the same girl I met 10 years ago
She has grown
Aging like sweet, sweet Appleton's Reserve
Blend

She seems to have been studying again
Reading some text about mass
communication
Scribbling notes
In her 52 page notebook
Sometimes if I'm lucky I might catch her
doodling
I've always admired that about her
Her unintentional flamboyance

ON BECOMING ROSE

Her love for words
How she read her way through life
From the hilly terrain of Clarendon where
there was no street light
To the bright lights of Kingston
I always knew she would go places

From rubber slippers to stiletto heels

If only you could see her now ...
She knew how proud you would be

I hope she knows that I love her now just as
how I loved her then
When all she had was the clothes on her back
How does one really water the rose that grew
from concrete?

Broken

There was a time I would've killed
To be her friend again when we argued
It was as if she was the only one who gets me
Everyone was the enemy and she my
superhero

Up up up and away
Here she comes to save the day
Someone else upsets me
Consumed with anger
Blinded by ignorance
Misguided by rumors
Trust no one
I followed her footsteps
Gullible Sally fell for whispers

Shh shhh someone's coming
Shh shh is anyone there?
Shh shh let's talk outside
She doesn't like you
He said this about you one time

ON BECOMING ROSE

Don't trust
I believed
I followed
My wings were clipped
You didn't warn me about yourself.

Her Season has Changed

I stayed home this time
Drank a bottle of wine
And listened to the sounds of Jazz & Blues
Then I danced to Mozart
I was in tuned with the classier me
Distancing myself from who or what saps my
energy
Or lowers my vibration ...
Dipped my grapes in caviar
Twirled my hair
It was as if I fell in love with myself
all over again
I fell in love with me
I fell in love with my own company
Learning things about me I didn't know existed
Learning things about me that excites me
More than anyone else
Where have I been all my life?????

Time Capsule

It's happening again
Feeling worked up
Trying to prove to you
And myself
That I've achieved
Certain things
Before the Age of Expiration
28

I just scrolled on Instagram
And saw another proposal
All my high school mates are either getting
married
Or having babies
And I'm here can't even catch a man
Or get one to commit
I'll be 28 next month
And although 2 years away from 30
It still feels like I'm about to turn 30

Have patience they say
Does that mean sit and wait?
Just allow things to flow?
Don't question anything
Relax and let it go?

30
I'm not ready for it
And It's fast-approaching
It makes you think of that
Career
Husband
Family
Children
Your own home

It makes you think
Ooh I should've had certain things already
It makes you think
My life should've been put together by now

Hey, can I have all my 20s back?

90s Love

Can you really give me that?
He scoffed and laughed.
If I ever touch you
You'd melt like ice, he said.
If only he could hear
The conversations I've been having
inside my head

Somehow he felt like he was the MAN
So I let him run with that
But one day I'll sit him down
And tell him what real love is like ...

And the type of love I like

90s Love

Sweet innocence
Before the Internet

Before Skype...
Those long love letters
Boom box outside my window
Playing my favourite song
Waking my parents up
And hearing the neighbours complain ...

No digital footprint
No online relationship status
No like/dislike button
Only privacy and mystery between us

So baby, why don't we use the Book of Atlas
When we go out on country trips
Instead of Google Maps
We'll have No one to track us
And study our whereabouts ...
Location: Off

No Twitter feeds to troll
No Instagram photos to be hurt by
Wondering why you're liking that girl's photos
so much
Oh when you keep leaving those Sony
Walkman tapes

ON BECOMING ROSE

Those Babyface Cassettes in my room
And that Brandy and Monica too!
Oh when you'll pick a flower in my garden
And give it to me
With the dirt stains hanging on the roots

I wanna love you if you can make me feel like
that ...

90s Love
Can you really give me that?

That tender love that Force MD's sang about
Where do I really get that at?

Introspection

Are you really giving yourselves that
Space and time
To heal
Or are you jumping from
One relationship to the next?
Do you fear being alone?
One should be happy with herself
Before she can be happy with someone else.
And be careful of the things
You speak over your life
You're not a mess.
You're not broken.
You are beautiful art
An inspiration to other women
Learning and discovering
Your divine purpose in this life.
You are a soul sister
A survivor
A voice and a speaker.

For Some Single Ladies:

I know you have lots of love to give
Because that's who you are.
But be careful.
Many will try to take advantage of that
Sparkling love bubble
You have inside.
They may think about us as naive,
Easy
A woman who sets no boundaries.
But be undoubtedly you
With a guard on your heart.
Never let anyone feel like they're being
chased.

Feeling for You No More

She said all that she could.

Sometimes I don't even know why she did
Because I felt like the love she gives
Was never being reciprocated

Sometimes I felt sorry for her
But then other times I admired
How brave she was.

She was never afraid
Just a girl who didn't get what
She deserved.

I congratulated her
The other day
Because she finally reached
That pinnacle

I prayed for her to reach
Where

She no longer cared
And lost all interest in people
Who were never worth it.

The First Bud

I stole one of your photos from your
Instagram page
Cropped out your friend Stephen
Saved it to my camera roll
Emailed it to Tiny at the Print Shop
He blew it up for me

I pasted it in my Notebook
And drew little hearts around it
Colour: Red
Ownership: Mine, mine, All mine
And it felt like Teenage Love all over
Again!
Just the thought of having you all for myself
makes me happy
Sharing was excluded
All of a sudden red petals started to bloom.

Coffee Love

I decided to write about you
Speaking about you wasn't enough
You came out of nowhere
You came into my life when I didn't know I
was ready for you

Ready for love
Ready for your love

Oh your love is like coffee
I can have it several ways but the taste never
dies

Monday: Black, no cream, no sugar - my kind
of bitter

Tuesday: Irish-inspired. It's like your skin is
dipped in whiskey and whipped cream

Wednesday: you're like my espresso, so

heavily brewed , rooted and grounded to your
African tribe, a leader of the pack, my wakanda
warrior and restless lover

Thursday: you're my coffee frappe, blended
with chocolate syrup poured all over
Skin to skin
Sometimes a little cinnamon would do
But you gotta know how much to use
A little inch here, a little inch there
Measurement's must be accurate if we want
to enjoy the taste

Fridays: the life of the party
Ristretto Baby!
Keep those shots coming!

Saturday and Sunday:
Your conversations, our conversations make
me whole
Just like sweet coffee all over again
The substance and consistency
Just keeps going
Keeps us brewing
Brew, my love.

Opening Up

I be moving too fast, fam

The last one told me I over-think too much
The one before that said I'm always in a hurry
And the one before him said
I'm always running

Shelly-Ann Fraser-Pryce ain't got nothing on
me!
Scared to hold on
Fear my grip is too tight
Ooh lose me
Loosen me
Can't stay one place too long
Comfortable in solace
Leave me in hiding

Opening up is just too hard.

The More Things Change, the More they Remain the Same

Is it really true what they say?
Yesterday I went back to the place

Where I grew up
14 years felt like 24
Time really does a lot
The streets haven't changed
Neither have the buildings
On my way there the sun felt like whips on my
back
Scorching every black layer on my skin

ON BECOMING ROSE

It was as if I was an orange being peeled in a
Stark green dress

Suspended by spaghetti straps
As I entered the street that was once called
home

I started to feel more and more like a stranger
As I walked persons on the road looked on
As if they're saying "a who she?"
I couldn't relate to anyone who lived
anywhere
Because I was always moving from house to
house

As I pushed open the gate
My sweaty palms made an imprint on the rusty
iron gate

Sticky

I looked around and saw that
A lot had changed but everything was still the
same
The outside bathroom was still there
The gully is still close to the back gate

The room was still there

The room where all of us slept hugging each
other on 6 sponges
It's like I never left.

On Finding Mr. Right

You're scrolling on Instagram and Facebook
And all you see is couples
Must be couples resort
They're either out having fun, getting married
or having babies
And u look at yourself in the mirror and ask
yourself

When is it gonna be my time?

You've been single for some time now
You've been through hell and back
Learned too many lessons
Dodged too many bullets
Buck your big toe countless amount of times
Shared your testimony with others
But still can't seem to find the right man

Or he can't seem to find you
Too many failed attempts
Starting over is too hard

Is something wrong with me?

God, are you there?

The Confrontation

Every morning I open up my eyes
To greet this place -
This place smelling of bloody needles
Disbelief
Clouded by death

I ask myself will I make it?

It's like when you arrive at the hospital door
All hope is left behind
All hell breaks loose
I tell mama don't cry
Because I don't wanna cry
Don't cry when strands of my hair are falling
out
Don't cry when... when my knees are failing
me
And my mind is weary

Don't cry because I'm flat-chested
The most beautiful women are not heavily
busted anyway

Don't cry when I'm losing weight rapidly
Don't cry because when you do it means that
I'll have to stop fighting
I'm here to say ...

Dear cancer
You really think you're in control
But one thing I'm sure of
You cannot mess with my soul
You cannot silence my prayers
And you cannot stifle my faith
Doc says I have 6 months to live
But I am not troubled

I will wait!

I will wait as there is a God
I will wait because I am more
than this outer shell
I will wait
And I will survive...

Under the Mango Tree

Sometimes I go outside to sit under the
mango tree
And listen to the birds
The dogs barking
Scattering rubbish on the street
Children playing in their yard
Enjoying innocence
Exploring the unknown
Sometimes I talk to God
And tell him about my day
What I could've done differently
And all the things I want to say
Sometimes I go there for peace

In nature's noise
Sometimes to reminisce and reflect
On yesterday's past
With the hope that tomorrow will be brighter

What will You Bring to the Table?

The first time I was asked this question
I was dating a man that could be my father
I was 23.
We were in his car, coming from his house
He pulled up in my drive-way
Then he asked ...
And I didn't know how to answer.
I felt that was his way of saying
I was too immature for him ...
Naive, impulsive and inexperienced.
It made me feel a little bit inferior

Because I didn't know how to respond
To his question -
What could I bring to what table?

ON BECOMING ROSE

Unemployed
Sharing room with my mom and sister
Exchanging body fluids
With a man who could not help me...

2 years later...

I'm working at a reputable organization
I'm listed as a staff member
I changed address
Have my own bed – my own place
Mom and sister migrated...

A message from Facebook messenger...
Can I have back your number?

I responded months after.
Gave him my new number.
He stopped by my new place.
Heard I was doing well.
Says he is happy for me.
He Can't Find A Stable relationship.
Since a girl screwed him over ...
He gave her everything.

I knew her name had to be karma.

He said he still had feelings for me
As they never died.
I told him mine died when we stopped talking.
I told him how much he hurt me 2 years ago
He should remember that he has a daughter.
He would have to fight to keep away men like
him from her.

But more importantly - if I took him back
What could he bring to the table?

He began to stutter.

So I assisted him...

Trust issues,
Problem with forgiveness
Lack of commitment...

I escaped.

Maturity

September 19, 2017
I apologized to love that day
I told her I was sorry
Sorry I thought she never existed
Sorry I said all those hurtful things to her and
about her

I went to visit an old friend.
She and I stopped talking awhile back
At the time I thought it was over and I
wouldn't have forgiven her
I thought there was no fixing it

But the spirit within me kept saying I needed
to see her
Called her work phone but she wasn't there
And I thought maybe that's not the right
medium
Then I went to her work place

Heard she wasn't there but will come in the
next day
When tomorrow came I decided to use my
lunch time again
Hopped out of the taxi
Walking up the stairs
Couldn't predict the outcome
Asked for her
Used my middle name at the security as fear
seeped in my pores

Who's that?

Tell her it's Carina I said to the guard

She said she's coming

I sat on the sofa waiting. At the back of my
mind I wondered if she was going to come
downstairs to me for real

Heard footsteps behind me and I looked up
and it was her. We both smiled. She Had That
Same Genuine smile I knew she had. It was
something that made you felt loved in her
presence

ON BECOMING ROSE

It was something I couldn't forget
Partly one of the reasons
I had to come see her
I remember how being around her used to be
like sweet slow poetry
Rare gem. Rare friend.

She sat down beside me and we both couldn't
stop smiling

Single denominator: a boy

Long story short she took my man
unintentionally
I had to forgive her and let it go
We spoke about it and played catch up
Time heals wounds

But have *my* wounds been fully healed ?

Do I need to play catch up with him as well?

Guards Up

For once she decided she didn't have to be all
that tough

That she could reveal her softer side and it
would be A-OK

And she would still be a lady

And she would still be winning

Guards down

The 2am Slot

I woke up at 2am
You promised you would come over
But another disappointing act
Because you didn't
Why do you always do this?
Build my hopes up to let them down back?

It's always this with you
And it's always that
Loyal to the excuses
I stay
You stay
Just for some temporary love
Temporary fun
Last time you told me
You were gonna climb my picket fences
Even if they were yay high

I believed it

Because I thought you were my better

half

Stuck somewhere between

Lonely and unhappy

Forgetting the fact that you made your bed

already with someone else

She's lying on it

Waiting for you to come home

And I'm just that girl on the sidelines

Side-eyeing you

Gosh, why am I so thirsty to be in love?

Thirsty for you

Why do I treat myself like this?

Why do I let you do me like this?

Why do I fall for these boys?

Ouch!

My head hurts

So bad when I think about the situation.

Quiet the Atmosphere

It was around 6pm
A Saturday
I had no errands to run
No meetings to attend
A day when I was all by myself
And to myself

I decided to chill at the nearest cafe
Hardly anyone was inside and
I got to sit at my favourite writing spot
In the corner of the sofa
The smell of coffee sweetened the air in the
room

Setting the tone for me to create stories in my
little black book
And stories I did write

Something different happened to me this time
I had forgotten about the past
Started writing happy thoughts
Creating happy memories

Suddenly there was a boy who liked me
And I liked him back
I kept thinking about him as I pen words to
paper

Words changing from hurt to love
From dark to flowery and all things pretty
To sunshine, horse-back riding and rose petals
To holding hands and making plans
From selfish to selfless
From long faces to happy faces
And adventurous places .

Quite the atmosphere
Quite the feeling.

Unfair Treatment

You met me as the sweet,
Caring guy
Nothing like you're used to

Go beyond the moon for you
Would give anything just to see you smile
Still nothing like you're used to

You told me the other day that I'm like your
boyfriend

And umm...

I really don't know if I should take it as a good
thing

We both know he doesn't respect you

And still you're lingering
Sleeping with
Hanging on to him

He doesn't walk with you in the park
Take you out for ice-cream
Or dinner
Like I do

Why the hell are you still with him?
He doesn't even see you
I thought cheating would've given you a
heads-up

Still you took him back with open arms
And open legs
Praying that he'll change
While I'm praying that you'll change

And see that all you need is a MAN

(Takes deep breath)

The man that I am.

Dirty 'ol Habit

I closed shop for awhile now

Knocks

He enters

I let him in again

Wished I could say no but my tongue won't let
me.

I dare me to find the strength over and over.

But that other part of me is still winning.

Only Love can Save Her

She forgot to clean her house
And all sorts of men showed up at her door
Wanting her body
As if she walked around with a
For Sale sign

She can't say no
She's so desperate to love
And to be loved
Trying so hard to save herself
From her former life
By falling in love

But it's not working
Every guy she dates,
Something is off
Or maybe it's her

She's frustrated

Relationships... they never work out
Because they come
And they take
And take
And she gives
And gives
Cheerfully

Taking Advantage

You pour me one more glass of wine

Trivento

Sweet Malbec

'Cause we're having a good, good time

And I don't wanna kill the vibe

But I have to.

I know what's on your mind.

"The room is hot"

Can you open up a window?

"Nah man, it's fine"

It wasn't.

"Let me use the bathroom"

My tiny frame could fit through the window.

Let's wait awhile before we go too far.

The Healing Process

Dear friend,
I had prayed for your healing
And while you're healing
I hope you will not hurt anyone.

Be gentle with yourself.
Will you?

Be patient with you.

Tings tek a little time
To unwind
To fall in line

Find your purpose.

Superwoman

Somehow I felt she needed
Some reassurance...

You're beautiful.
She needed to hear that.
She had to pause in order to soak those lines
in.
It wasn't as if she didn't know who she was
And what she was about.

But she had been so caught up
Outside
That she did not remember to look in the
mirror lately.
Too busy being busy
Too busy to find time for herself.
Busy trying to save the world.

Thank God for Maturity

Dear friend,
I'm happy we're no longer
At that place.
The Toxic City.
We are so beyond that - so far away.
That not even the sky can catch us now.
We have cleansed our spirits and
Allowed forgiveness to seep in.

That was beautiful.
That we were able to change at such a time as
this

Thank God for Maturity.

Apologies are Still a Thing

I wore a leopard dress today
Long, flowing ...
Accentuating my curves
Tied around my neck
Silver hoop earrings
Oh I wish you could've seen me

I wish I saw you and you were telling me how
beautiful I looked and how amazing I am

I'm coming from a friend's house and no he
and I ain't like that
I guess it was a cheap excuse to watch my
favourite new show on Netflix or an excuse to
take my mind off you for a couple a hours

An excuse to not look at my phone every 5
seconds to see when you come online

ON BECOMING ROSE

But you were a no-show
That made my night even more depressing.
I'm sorry.
I went to your work place
Was told you weren't there
I seemed to be on some stalker shit because
I called your uncle who said he didn't hear
from you

Oh where oh where could you be, Daniel?
...
I guess that's what I needed in my life
A real man to love me.

Looking for Love

My friend and one of your God-mothers is out
there looking
Praying for your father to show his face

Praying for the one who she and I will both
call 'husband'

She and I are too much alike.
Similar personalities
Similar interests

She prays that we both find our husbands and
stop wasting time
with men that aren't for us

I pray for the same thing too.
My son, there are days I feel like I'm cursed or

I'm trapped.
The men that approach me are either in my
age group
and are immature
or older and in a relationship

The ones that are older and in a relationship
are usually the nicest

But I don't wish to entertain anyone from
either categories.

I want someone that will complement me

Someone who is hand-picked by God.

Lessons to Value

I think she loved the drama
She knows he ain't good for her
But went ahead with the relationship anyway

I think it's the excitement she craved
The back and forth
The tug o' war
She loved it

She wasn't used to calmness
She wasn't used to a man loving her from afar
She wasn't used to a man only kissing her on
her forehead
It was like someone speaking a different
language to her

ON BECOMING ROSE

She knew she deserved to be happy
She knew that most her relationships did not
exude happiness
She knew that a happy relationship
was one that is beautiful and healthy

But your mother was always stubborn
The g.o.a.t who did not always listen

And the g.o.a.t who kept on getting up when
she falls

I pray you understand her
Appreciate her
And love her with all your heart

I pray you show Respect to all females
Stand up for what is right
Take no less than what you deserve
Take no disrespect from any.
Never put your hands on a woman.

I pray your relationship will be healthy and
filled with happiness, when you have a wife.

And when you make that woman your wife, I
pray both of you love each other
Pray for each other
Pray with each other
Build each other up
Communicate to each other with love
Ride through the storms together
Be the couple others can emulate

Put God first

I pray you value these lessons.

The Emergency Pill

My son, my daughter
This could be you

But your mom kept Playing Never Have I Ever
Too many thoughts in my head
What ifs
Buts
People will say this
People will say that

It's just one pill Tiffany
All it takes is a glass of water
And
Your gut

(Sighs)

What if it's my only chance to...
Then again I can't have it
He's not ready for
I'm not ready for
She's definitely not ready for
The Emergency Pill story.

(Gulps)

Stepping Into Your New Season

I cut the calluses from her feet today.

I had to remind her that the dead things of her
life had to go -

That their expiration date had come
and it was now time for her to step into her
new season.

All I want is to see her WIN and today was the
day to start.

www.ingramcontent.com/pod-product-compliance
Lightning Source LLC
Chambersburg PA
CBHW071059090426
42737CB00013B/2393

* 9 7 8 9 7 6 8 2 4 0 9 6 5 *